春雨惊春清谷天
夏满芒夏暑相连
秋处露秋寒霜降
冬雪雪冬小大寒

本教材为 2016 年度教育部哲学社会科学研究重大课题攻关项目
“中国书法文化国际传播的理论与实践研究”（16JZD031）阶段性成果

二十四节气

風調雨順

Winter: Season with Timely Breeze and Rain for Crop Raising

The Twenty-four Solar Terms

主编：周斌 周佳楠
Editor-in-chief: ZHOU Bin, ZHOU Jianan
副主编：Roy Ye 尹冬民
Associate Editor: Roy Ye, YIN Dongmin
插图：孙凌雁
Illustrator:SUN Lingyan
书法：盛兰军
Calligraphy: SHENG Lanjun
翻译：胡子曦 Christina Peters
Translators: HU Zixi，Christina Peters
封面题字：Roy Ye
Calligraphy on the cover: Roy Ye

华东师范大学出版社

Hi, Nini, the weather is getting cold and it has snowed. Is it time to start a new solar term?

You are right, Jerry. Now it's Beginning of Winter, which means the end of autumn. In winter, it's going to snow in a lot of places in China. There is an old Chinese saying, "A timely heavy snow promises a good harvest in the coming year." Snowing represents a good sign!

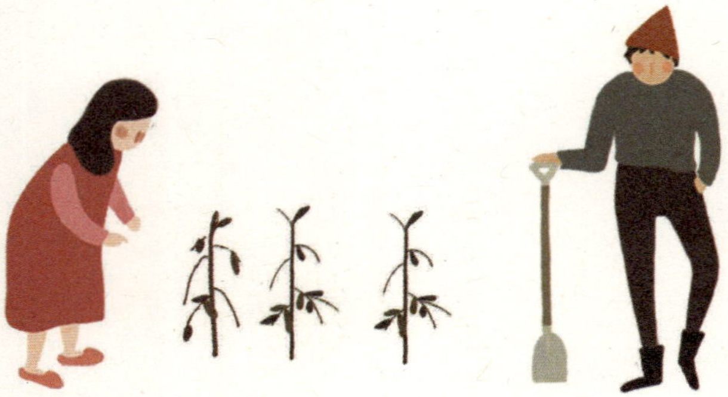

妮妮，最近天气好冷啊，已经下雪了，是不是又要开始新的节气了？

杰瑞，你说得没错，现在是立冬时节，秋天结束了，冬天要来了。冬季中国好多地方都会下雪，古人说“瑞雪兆丰年”，下雪可是个好兆头呢！

二十四节气与十二星座对照图

The table of the Twenty-four Solar Terms and the corresponding astrological signs

Contents

The Symphony of Winter

目　录

冬季乐章

立冬

Beginning of Winter
Li Dong

The story of **Beginning of Winter**

Important facts about Beginning of Winter

Beginning of Winter comes first in winter between the 7th and 8th of November. Beginning of Winter, as its name shows, is considered to be the start of winter. From this point to the next turning point of the climate, crops will be harvested and preserved. After Beginning of Winter, the precipitation sharply decreases. Meanwhile certain meteorological phenomena, like sleet, mist and graupel, appear.

Changes after Beginning of Winter

Orchids bloom; fruit trees need to be trimmed.

Soil as well as water surface freezes.

Animals begin hibernating; pheasants rest in the forest.

立冬大事记

立冬是冬季的第一个节气，时间点在每年的11月7～8日之间。立冬预示着冬季的到来。在这个节气，农作物收割后被储存起来。进入立冬后，降水显著减少，但是雨夹雪、雾、霰等天气现象开始出现。

立冬变化

兰花开放，果树剪枝。
土地封冻，水面结冰。
动物冬眠，雉鸟归林。

跟着妮妮学一学
Learning Chinese calligraphy with Nini

篆书 (zhuan shu) | Seal script

"立"字的本义是"站立"。篆书"立"的字形像一个人分开两腿，站立在地上。

"立" means "to stand". The seal script of "立" resembles a man standing straight on the ground with his legs apart.

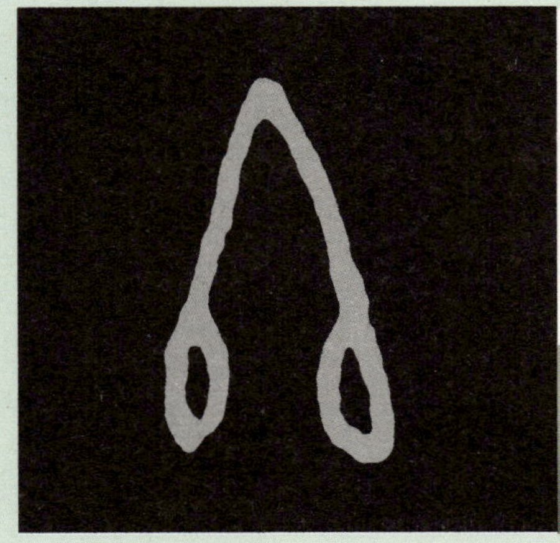

篆书"冬"字的字形像在一条绳子的两端各打上一个结，表示终结的意思。后来"冬"字表示一个纪时周期的结束，即四季的终结——冬季。

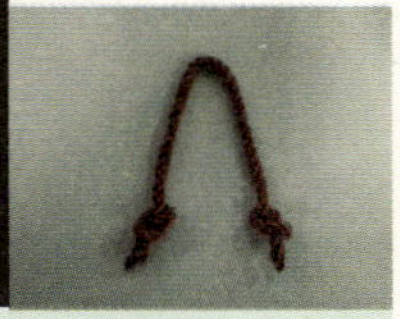

The seal script of "冬" resembles a rope with a knot at each end which implies the end of something. Later it evolved to mean the end of a period of time. Winter is at the end of a year. Thus, "冬"has come to mean winter.

跟着杰瑞写一写

Practicing calligraphy with Jerry

楷书（kai shu）| Regular script

在学写"立冬"之前，我们先来学习书法中一些常见的基本笔画。之后大家可以举一反三进行练习。

Before we start writing "立冬", let's learn some fundamental strokes in Chinese calligraphy first. Then you will be able to apply them to your later practice.

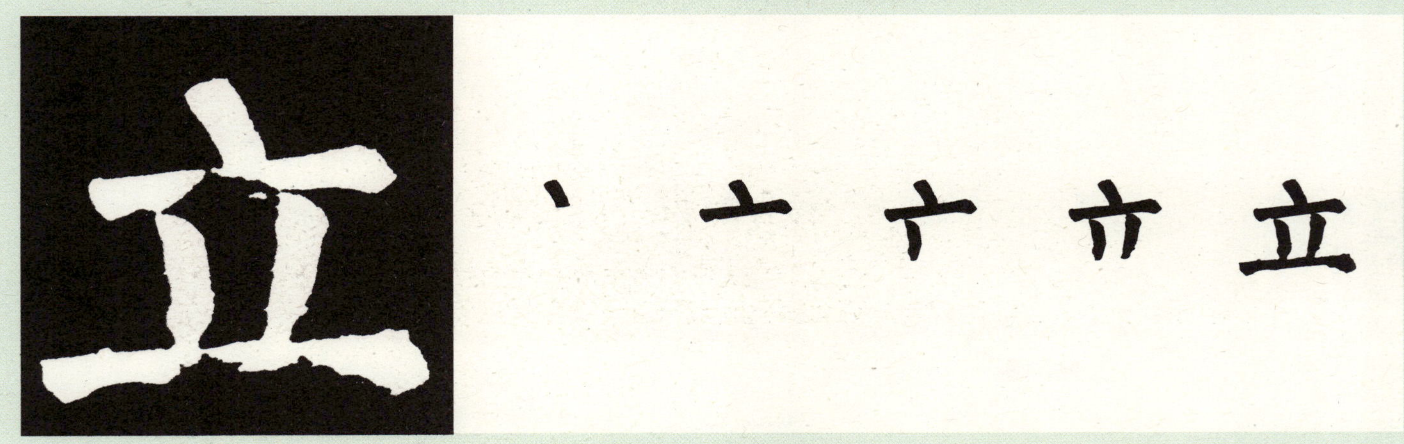

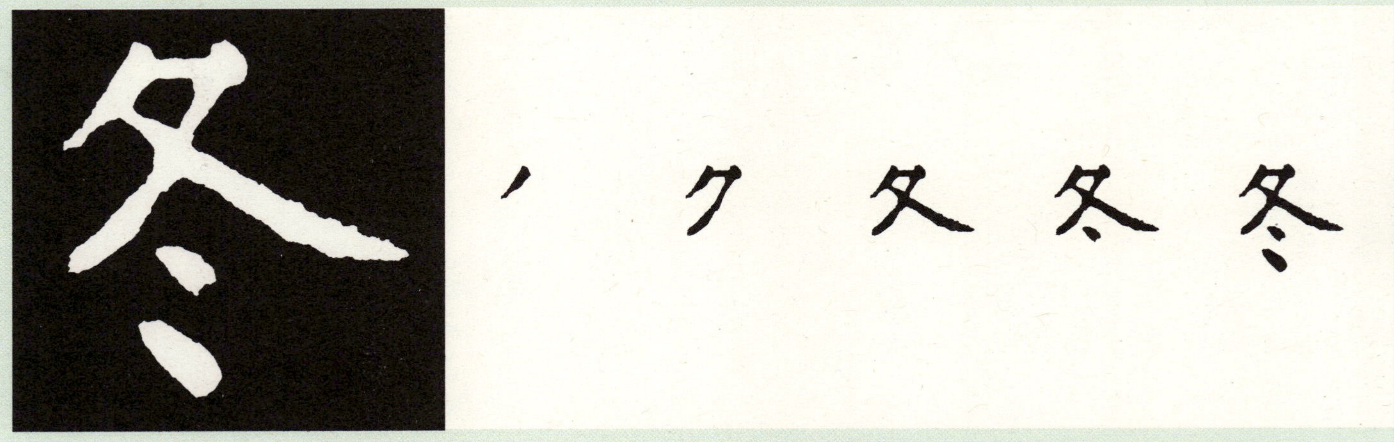

剪一剪、画一画

Paper cutting and graphic design

Make a gift with Chinese characters "立冬"

剪剪画画

做立冬的礼物

跟着妮妮和杰瑞做送给朋友的礼物

Let's make some gifts for our friends with Nini and Jerry

Paper cutting by Nini

妮妮的剪纸

Graphic designed by Jerry

杰瑞的画

猜一猜、说一说

Let's make a guess

Let's make a guess with Nini and Jerry

与妮妮和杰瑞一起猜一猜

与“立冬”对应的是哪个星座？

Which astrological sign corresponds to Beginning of Winter?

Let's have a competition with Nini and Jerry

与妮妮和杰瑞一起比赛

说出与“冬”有关的词语

Try to say as many words as you can that are relevant to “冬”

小雪

Light Snow

Xiao Xue

Important facts about Light Snow

The story of **Light Snow**

Light Snow comes between the 22nd and 23rd of November. From the point of Light Snow, the temperature starts to drop gradually. The temperature in the north of China can fall below zero degrees centigrade. And snow starts to fall, however not in large amounts. This is how the name of Light Snow comes about. Snow in this period of time is beneficial to winter wheat and other crops.

Changes after Light Snow

Daffodils bloom; chrysanthemums wither.

Rainbows never appear; the first snow in a year falls.

People start to store vegetables and salt pork.

小雪的故事

小雪大事记

小雪的时间点是在每年的11月22～23日之间。小雪时节，气温逐渐下降，北方地区气温逐步降到0℃以下，开始出现降雪，但雪量一般不大，所以被称为小雪。这个时期的降雪对冬小麦等农作物的生长十分有益。

小雪变化

水仙花开，菊花枯萎。
彩虹不见，初雪飘飞。
贮藏蔬菜，腌制腊肉。

跟着妮妮学一学
Learning Chinese calligraphy with Nini

篆书（zhuan shu）| Seal script

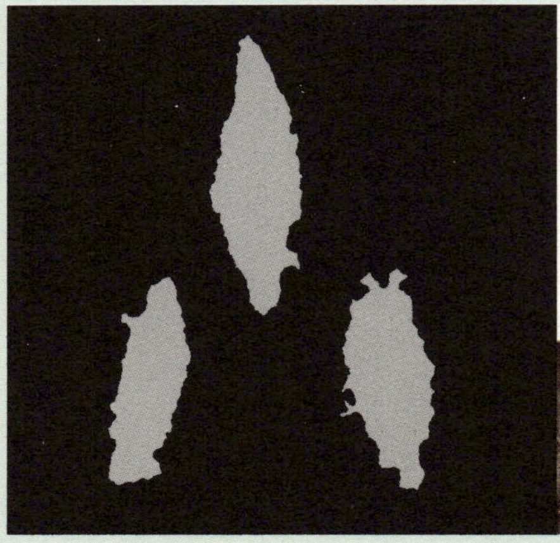

篆书"小"字从字形上看像数颗细小的沙粒散落四周，表示细小、细微的意思。

The seal script of "小" resembles several tiny grains of sand scattered around, which indicates smallness or subtlety.

篆书"雪"字由"雨"和"彗"两个部分组成，表示雪是由天空中的雨水凝结而成的飘落到地面的冰晶。

The seal script of "雪" consists of "雨" and "彗", which implies that snow, shaped as the ice crystals, falling onto the ground, comes from frozen raindrops.

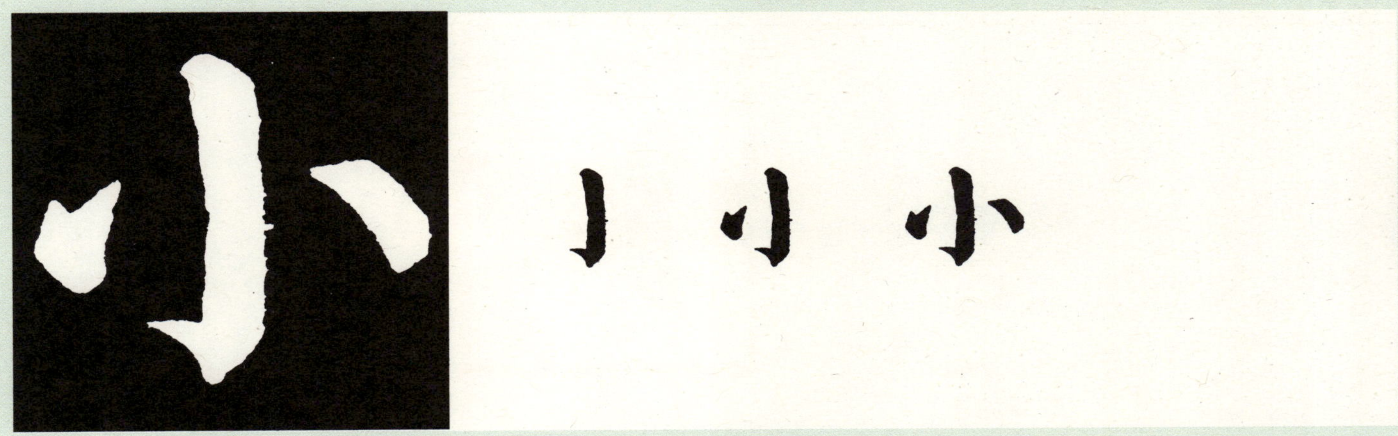
小

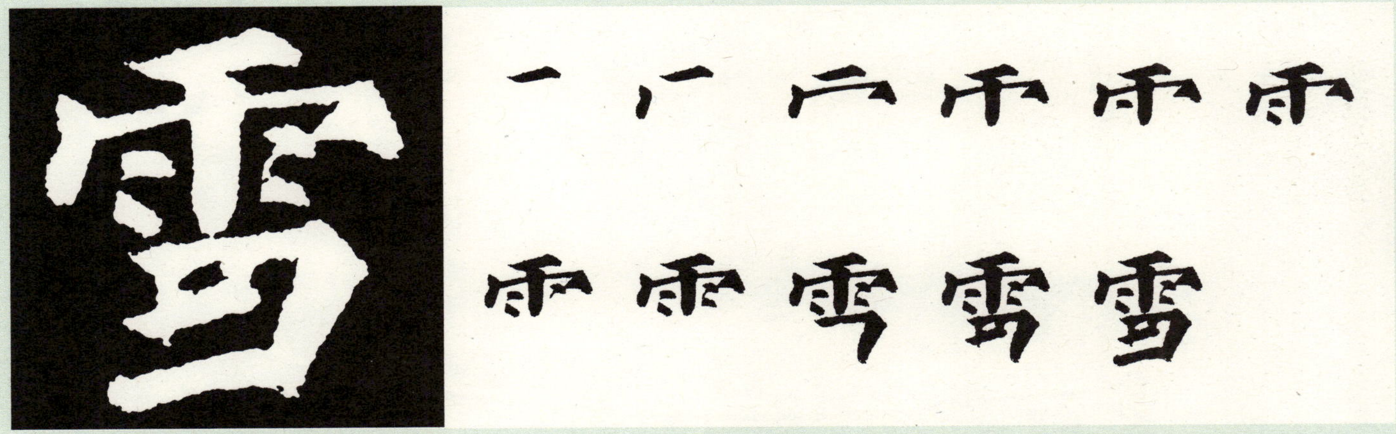
雪

Make a gift with Chinese characters “小雪”

剪剪画画 做小雪的礼物

跟着妮妮和杰瑞
做送给朋友的
礼物

Let’s make some gifts for our friends with Nini and Jerry

剪一剪、画一画

Paper cutting and graphic design

Paper cutting by Nini

妮妮的剪纸

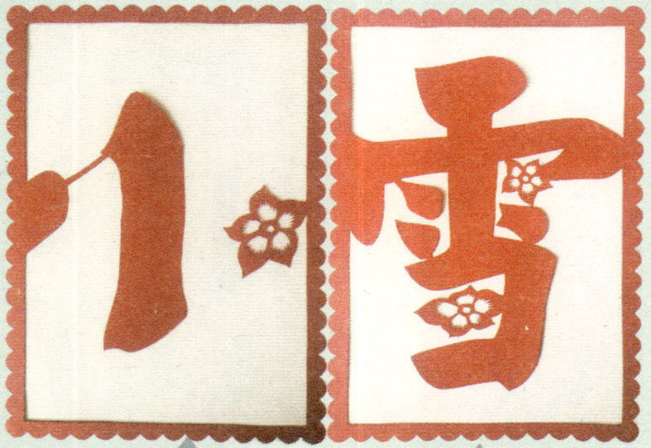

Graphic designed by Jerry

杰瑞的画

猜一猜、说一说

Let's make a guess

Let's make a guess with Nini and Jerry

与妮妮和杰瑞一起猜一猜

与“小雪”对应的是哪个星座？

Which astrological sign corresponds to Light Snow?

Let's have a competition with Nini and Jerry

与妮妮和杰瑞一起比赛

说出与“小”有关的词语

Try to say as many words as you can that are relevant to “小”.

大雪

Heavy Snow

Da Xue

The story of

Heavy Snow

Important facts about Heavy Snow

Heavy Snow comes between the 7th and 8th of December every year. From this point, the temperature falls lower and lower. Snow gets heavier and heavier and can stay on the ground for a while. What's more, a covering of snow benefits wheat and other crops by maintaining their temperature throughout the cold winter and killing worm eggs. Since snow plays a significant role in agriculture, there is an old Chinese saying, "A timely heavy snow promises a good harvest in the coming year."

Changes after Heavy Snow

The whole world is covered by ice and snow; the auspicious snow falls fast down.
Flying squirrels stop squeaking; tigers start their courtship rituals.
Litchi trees sprout; sasanqua and camellias bloom.

大雪的故事

大雪大事记

大雪的时间点是在每年的12月7日～8日之间。大雪时节，气温越来越低，降雪量越来越大，下雪之后地面开始有积雪。这个时期的积雪会覆盖在小麦等农作物上，帮助它们保温，还能够冻死越冬的虫卵，对农业生产有十分重要的作用，因此中国民间有“瑞雪兆丰年”的说法。

大雪变化

千里冰封，瑞雪纷飞。
鶡鼠不鸣，老虎求偶。
荔挺出芽，茶梅花开。

跟着妮妮学一学
Learning Chinese calligraphy with Nini

篆书 (zhuan shu) | Seal script

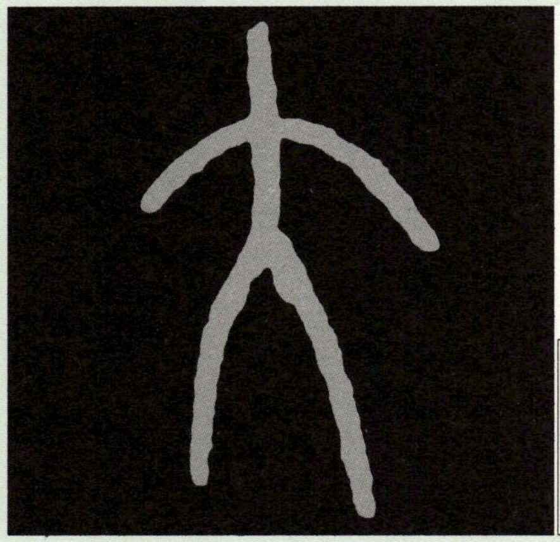

篆书"大"字像一个张开双臂和双腿的顶天立地的人。它的本义是天大，地大，人也大。

The seal script of "大" is like a man stretching out arms and legs to hold the heaven and the earth. It originally means the sky is wide, the earth is broad, and so is the human being.

篆书"雪"字由"雨"和"彗"两个部分组成，表示雪是由天空中的雨水凝结而成的飘落到地面的冰晶。

The seal script of "雪" consists of "雨" and "彗", which implies that snow, shaped as the ice crystals, falling onto the ground, comes from frozen raindrops.

楷书（kai shu）| Regular script

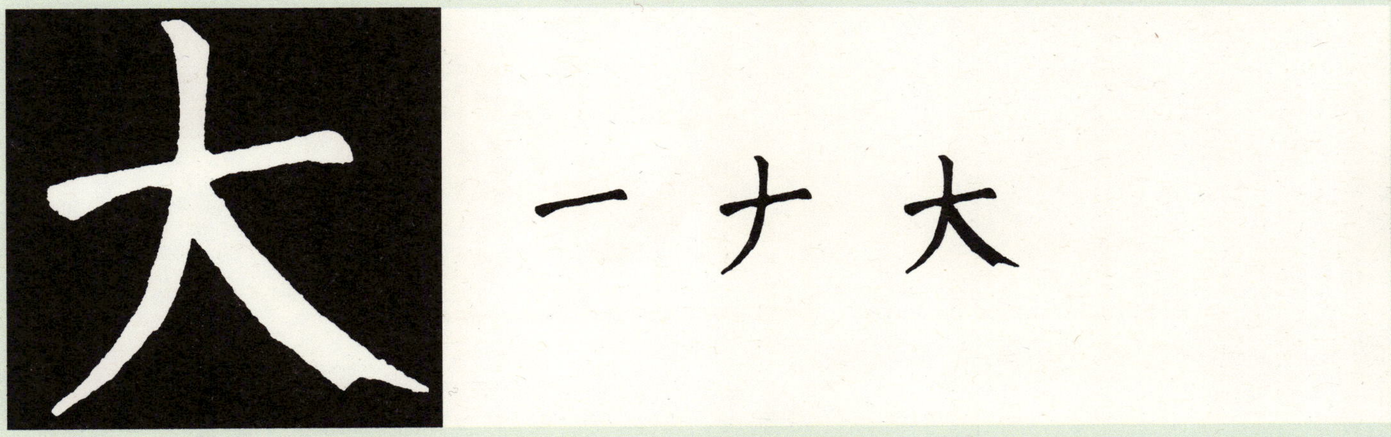

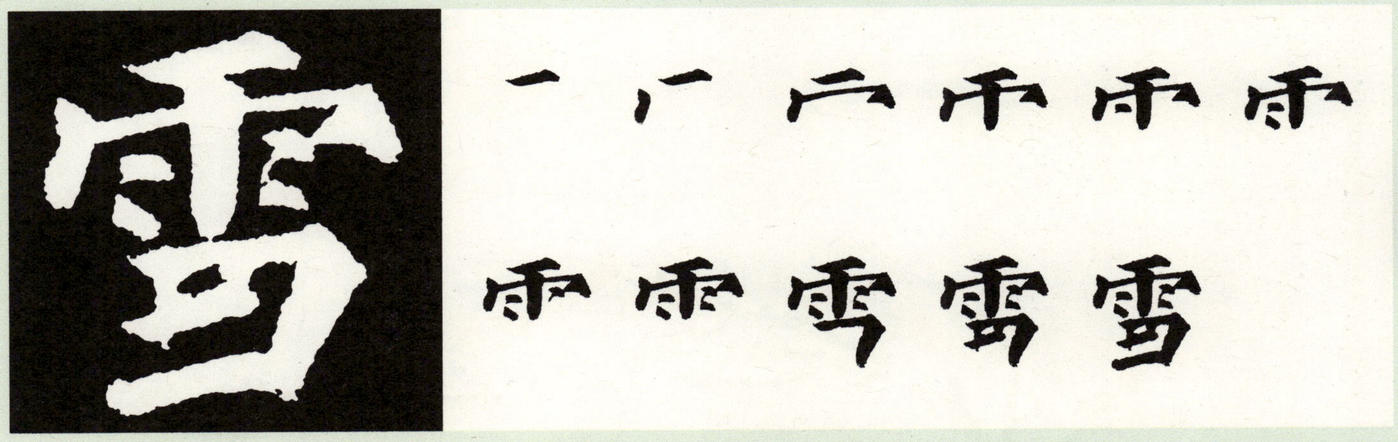

剪一剪、画一画

Paper cutting and graphic design

Make a gift with Chinese characters “大雪”

剪剪画画

做大雪的礼物

跟着妮妮和杰瑞
做送给朋友的
礼物

Let's make some gifts for our friends with Nini and Jerry

Paper cutting by Nini

妮妮的剪纸

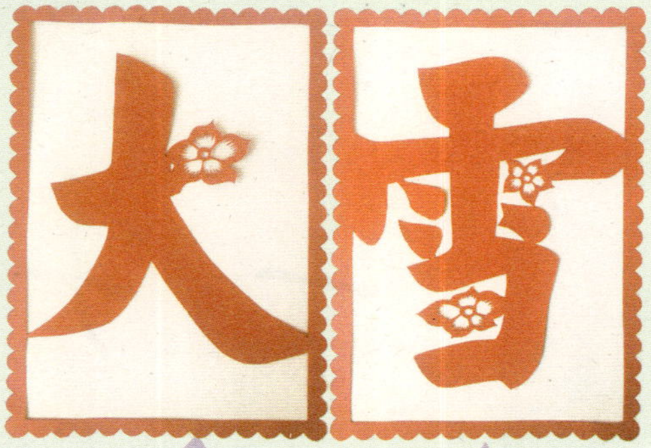

Graphic designed by Jerry

杰瑞的画

猜一猜、说一说

Let's make a guess

Let's make a guess with Nini and Jerry

与妮妮和杰瑞一起猜一猜

与“大雪”对应的是哪个星座？

Which astrological sign corresponds to Heavy Snow?

Let's have a competition with Nini and Jerry

与妮妮和杰瑞一起比赛

说出与“雪”有关的词语

Try to say as many words as you can that are relevant to “雪”

冬至

Winter Solstice
Dong Zhi

Important facts about Winter Solstice

The story of **Winter Solstice**

Winter Solstice, a significant turning point of the climate in a year, comes between the 21st and 23rd of December. On the day of Winter Solstice, the sun's angle of incidence turns perpendicular to the Tropic of Capricorn, and the North Hemisphere has the shortest day and the longest night of the year. After Winter Solstice comes the most rigid cold period of time in a year, thus Chinese name it as "Shu Jiu Han Tian". In ancient China, people considered 9 days to be one unit. The most rigid cold period of time of the year lasts for 9 units, which adds up to 81 days in total. Then the poplar blossom is in bloom and the weather begins to get warm again.

Changes after Winter Solstice

Camellias bloom; brooks babble in the mountains.
Earthworms still curl up underground; milu deers shed their antlers.
People make dumplings and tangyuan.

冬至大事记

冬至的时间点是在每年的12月21～23日之间。冬至在中国传统中是十分重要的节气，这一天太阳直射南回归线，北半球经历一年里黑夜最长、白天最短的一天。冬至过后将迎来一年中最寒冷的阶段，民间俗称“数九寒天”。从冬至这天开始数，每九天为一个“九”，数完九九八十一天，就算“九”尽了，“九尽杨花开”，天气就暖和了。

冬至变化

山茶花开，山泉流动。
蚯蚓蜷缩，麋鹿褪角。
煮煮饺子，包包汤圆。

跟着妮妮学一学

Learning Chinese calligraphy with Nini

篆书 (zhuan shu) | Seal script

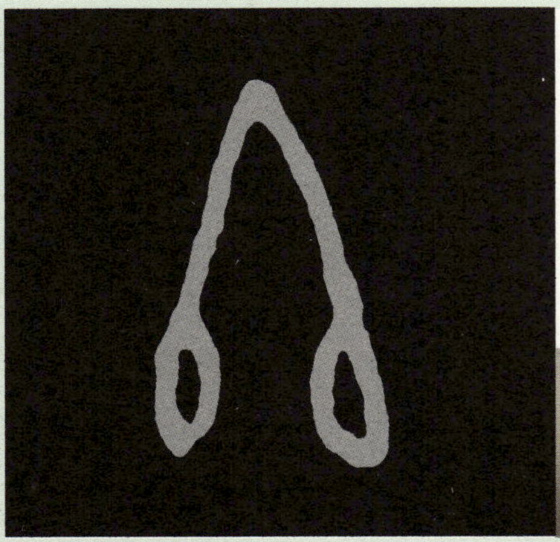

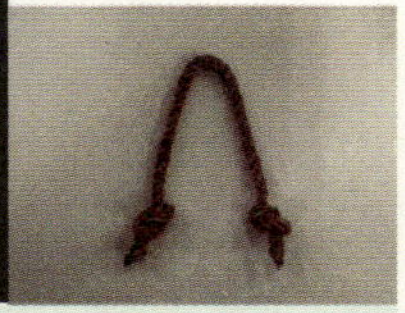

篆书"冬"字的字形像在一条绳子的两端各打上一个结，表示终结的意思。"冬"字后来表示一个纪时周期的结束，即四季的终结——冬季。

The seal script of "冬" resembles a rope with a knot at each end which implies the end of something. Later it evolved to mean the end of a period of time. Winter is at the end of a year. Thus, "冬"has come to mean winter.

篆书"至"是会意字，它的字形像飞鸟从高处落到地上，其本义是到达。

The seal script of "至" is an associative compound, which means readers can understand its meaning by connecting the shape of the character. The character looks like a bird flying down from a high place and thus it means "arriving".

楷书（kai shu）| Regular script

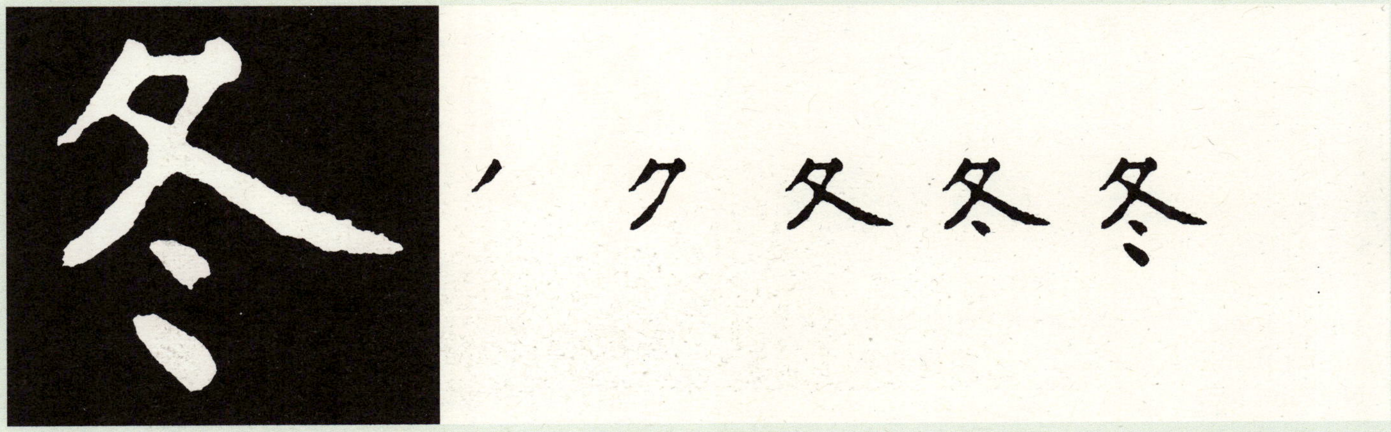

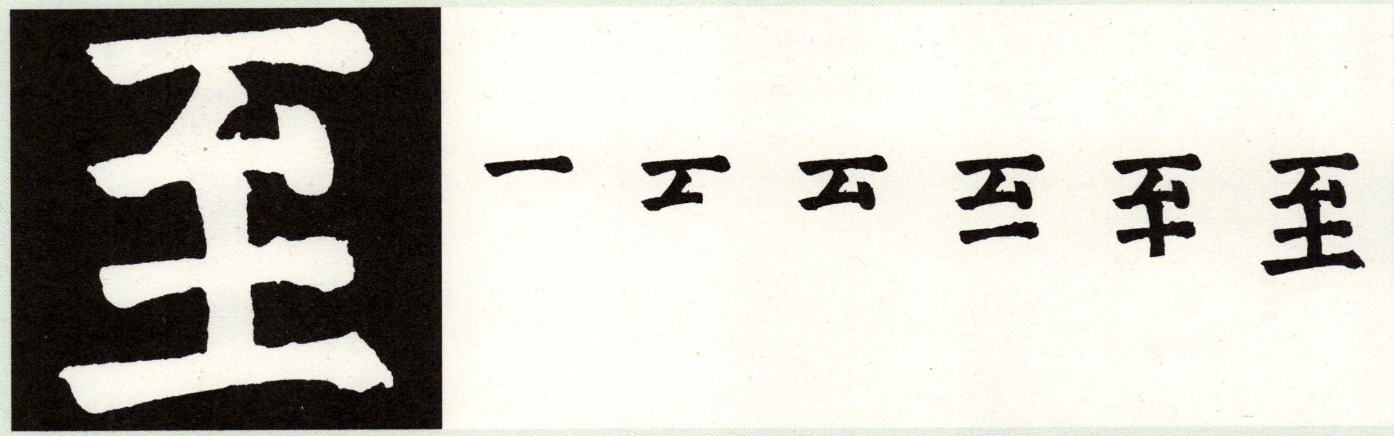

剪一剪、画一画

Paper cutting and graphic design

Make a gift with Chinese characters “冬至”

剪剪画画
做冬至的礼物

跟着妮妮和杰瑞做送给朋友的礼物

Let’s make some gifts for our friends with Nini and Jerry

Paper cutting by Nini
妮妮的剪纸

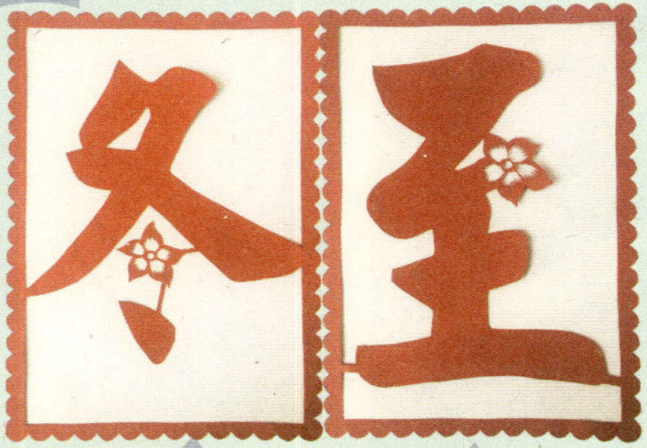

Graphic designed by Jerry
杰瑞的画

猜一猜、说一说

Let's make a guess

Let's make a guess with Nini and Jerry

与妮妮和杰瑞一起猜一猜

与“冬至”对应的是哪个星座？

Which astrological sign corresponds to Winter Solstice?

Let's have a competition with Nini and Jerry

与妮妮和杰瑞一起比赛

说出与“至”有关的词语

Try to say as many words as you can that are relevant to “至”

小寒

Lesser Cold

Xiao Han

The story of

Lesser Cold

Important facts about Lesser Cold

Lesser Cold comes between the 5th and 7th of January every year. It indicates the coldest period of time in a year comes after Lesser Cold. There is an old saying in China that goes, "The days of the 'Sanjiu period' are the coldest days," which just comes after Lesser Cold. This point is also the beginning of the last month in Chinese lunar calendar called "La Yue".

Changes after Lesser Cold

Calyx canthus come into full blossom; wild geese migrate to the north.
Magpies start to build their new nests; pheasants start to crow.
People make porridge with eight ingredients; people also pickle the heads of garlic.

Tips

People make Laba porridge with eight ingredients, such as red dates, lotus seeds, dried longans, red beans, millet, rice, peanuts and the fruits of Chinese wolfberry.

小寒大事记

小寒的时间点是在每年的1月5～7日之间。进入小寒标志着一年中最为寒冷的日子到来了。俗语说"冷在三九"，"三九"就在小寒节气之后，至此我们也进入了农历一年中的最后一个月份"腊月"。

小寒变化

腊梅盛开，大雁北飞。
喜鹊筑巢，雉鸟鸣叫。
煮腊八粥，腌腊八蒜。

小贴士

人们常用八种食材熬制腊八粥，食材包括红枣、莲子、桂圆、红豆、小米、大米、花生和枸杞。

跟着妮妮学一学
Learning Chinese calligraphy with Nini

篆书 (zhuan shu) | Seal script

篆书"小"字从字形上看像数颗细小的沙粒散落四周，表示细小、细微的意思。

The seal script of "小" resembles several tiny grains of sand scattered around, which indicates smallness or subtlety.

篆书"寒"字外框表示房屋，下面是冰，字的中间是人在草堆里的样子。整个字表示在冰冷天气人躲进屋子里，钻入草堆中避寒，意思是寒冷。

The outer part of the seal script of "寒" stands for shelter, the bottom part stands for ice and the middle part resembles an image of a man in the rick. The whole character indicates a man who stays in the house and burrows himself into the rick in order to keep away from the coldness under the freezing weather. It means freezing coldness.

跟着杰瑞写一写

Practicing calligraphy with Jerry

楷书（kai shu）| Regular script

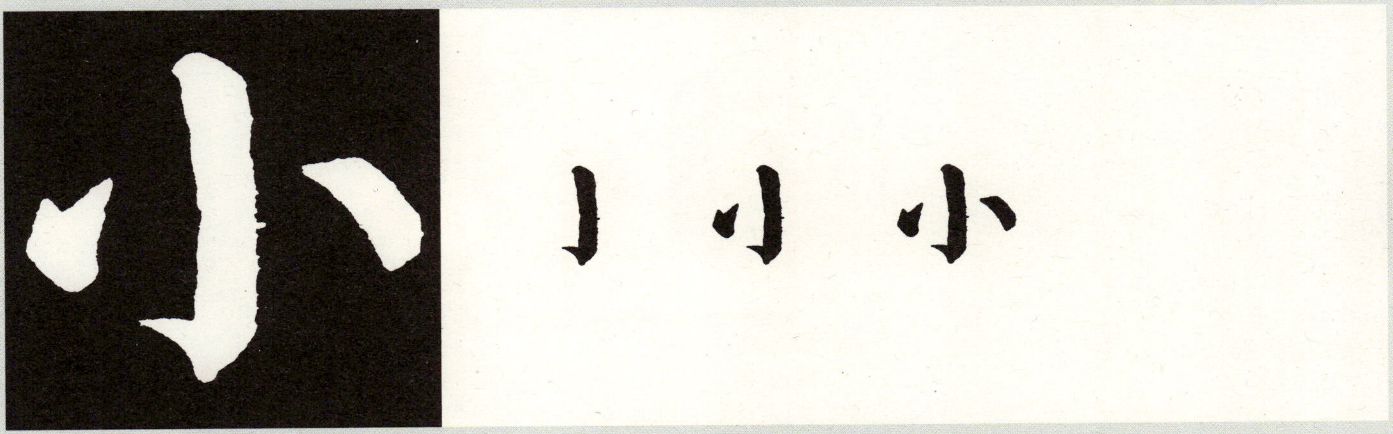

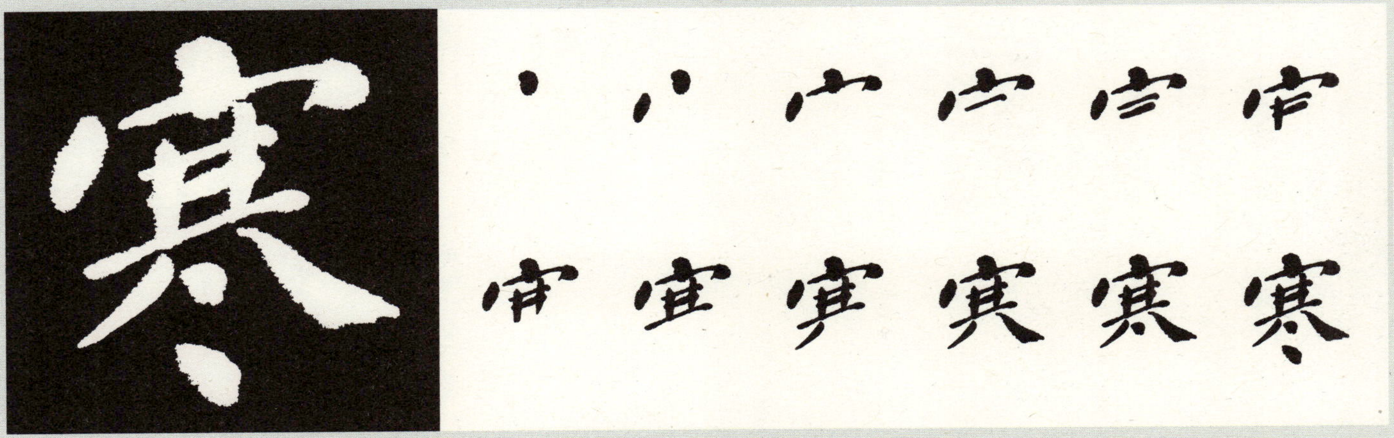

Make a gift with Chinese characters “小寒”

剪剪画画
做小寒的礼物

跟着妮妮和杰瑞做送给朋友的礼物

Let’s make some gifts for our friends with Nini and Jerry

剪一剪、画一画

Paper cutting and graphic design

Paper cutting by Nini
妮妮的剪纸

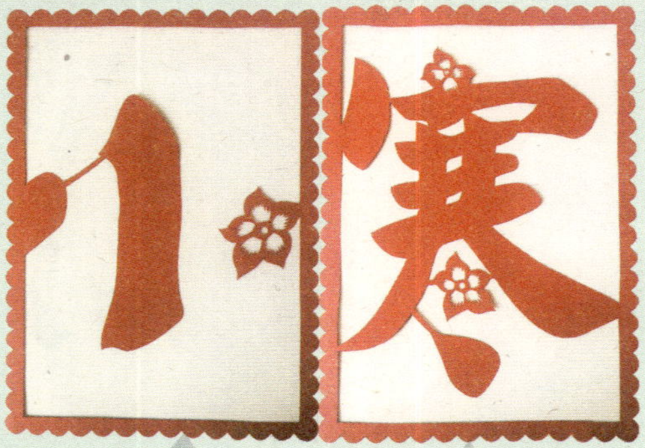

Graphic designed by Jerry
杰瑞的画

猜一猜、说一说

Let's make a guess

Let's make a guess with Nini and Jerry

与妮妮和杰瑞一起猜一猜

与"小寒"对应的是哪个星座？

Which astrological sign corresponds to Lesser Cold?

Let's have a competition with Nini and Jerry

与妮妮和杰瑞一起比赛

说出与"寒"有关的词语

Try to say as many words as you can that are relevant to "寒"

大寒

Greater Cold

Da Han

The story of **Greater Cold**

Important facts about Greater Cold

Greater Cold, which is the last solar term of winter, comes between the 19th and 21st of January. It is the coldest time and the precipitation reaches its lowest point in this period of time. After Greater Cold, Chinese New Year is just around the corner. Everyone is busy making New Year purchases, writing New Year Scrolls, cleaning houses and preparing delicious food for the coming new year. Then, we will begin another cycle of 24 turning points of the climate in a brand new year.

Changes after Greater Cold

Rivers freeze; snow accumulates on the ground.

Chickens hatch their eggs; birds of prey become more violent.

People clean their houses and get ready for Chinese New Year.

大寒的故事

大寒大事记

大寒是冬季的最后一个节气，大寒的时间点在每年的1月19～21日之间。大寒时节是一年中最为寒冷的阶段，也是一年中降水最少的时节。过了大寒，农历新年即将到来，大家都忙着买年货、写春联、打扫房屋、准备庆贺新年的美食。大寒之后，我们又将迎来新的一年的节气轮回。

大寒变化

江河冰封，积雪皑皑。
雏鸡孵化，征鸟厉疾。
打扫房屋，迎接新年。

跟着妮妮学一学
Learning Chinese calligraphy with Nini

篆书 (zhuan shu) | Seal script

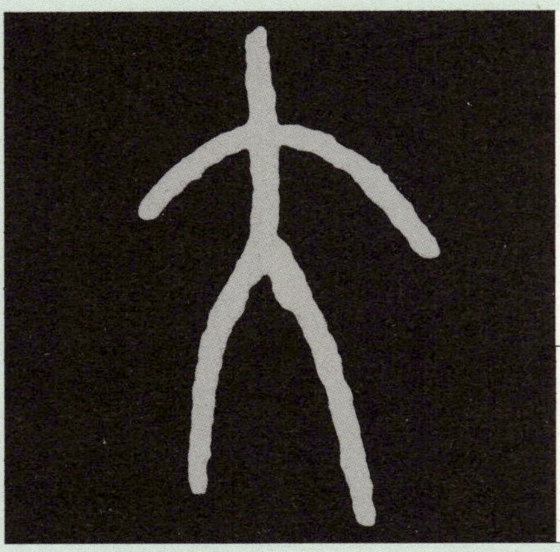

篆书"大"字像一个张开双臂和双腿的顶天立地的人。它的本义是天大，地大，人也大。

The seal script of "大" is like a man stretching out arms and legs to hold the heaven and the earth. It originally means the sky is wide, the earth is broad, and so is the human being.

篆书"寒"字外框表示房屋，下面是冰，字的中间是人在草堆里的样子。整个字表示在冰冷天气人躲进屋子里，钻入草堆中避寒，意思是寒冷。

The outer part of the seal script of "寒" stands for shelter, the bottom part stands for ice and the middle part resembles an image of a man in the rick. The whole character indicates a man who stays in the house and burrows himself into the rick in order to keep away from the coldness under the freezing weather. It means freezing coldness.

跟着杰瑞写一写

Practicing calligraphy with Jerry

楷书（kai shu）| Regular script

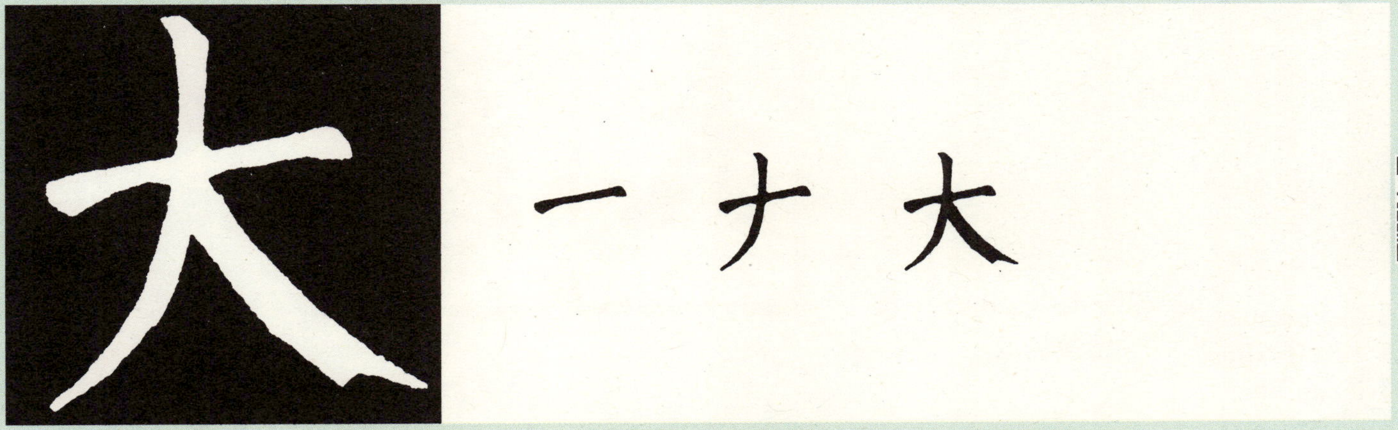

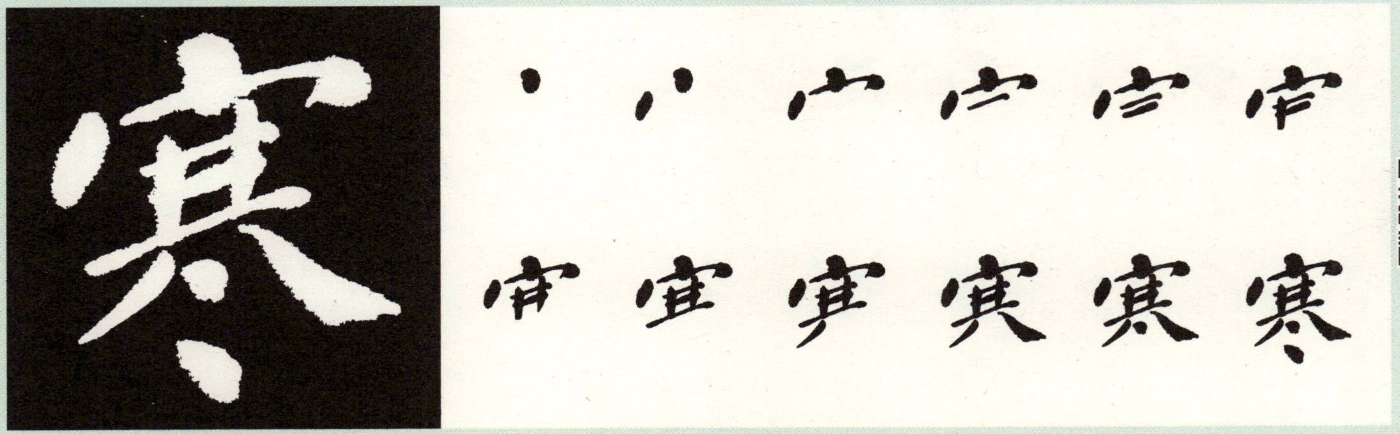

Make a gift with Chinese characters “大寒”

剪剪画画

做大寒的礼物

跟着妮妮和杰瑞
做送给朋友的
礼物

Let’s make some gifts for our friends with Nini and Jerry.

剪一剪、画一画

Paper cutting and graphic design

Paper cutting by Nini
妮妮的剪纸

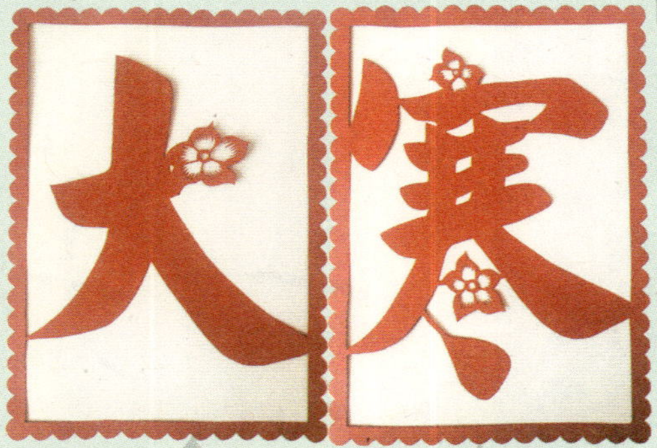

Graphic designed by Jerry
杰瑞的画

猜一猜、说一说

Let's make a guess

Let's make a guess with Nini and Jerry

与妮妮和杰瑞一起猜一猜

与“大寒”对应的是哪个星座？

Which astrological sign corresponds to Greater Cold?

Let's have a competition with Nini and Jerry

与妮妮和杰瑞一起比赛

说出与“大”有关的词语

Try to say as many words as you can that are relevant to “大”

后记

自2014年完成了“书法小联合国”文化特色教材《十二生肖我来写》之后，一直收到不同国家各级学校老师发来的邮件，询问是否可以买到课程的示范录像，也有老师与家长鼓励我继续编写一些有趣的关于中国传统文化的书法教材。

编写海外书法文化启蒙教材是一件十分艰难的事，看起来只是一本几十页的小书，要编写好绝非一日之功。首先要找到一个好的素材，之后要在不同的文化语境中反复进行教学实验，咨询各方专家的意见，最后方能定稿。多年来，“书法小联合国”国际系列教材编写的目标是：教材既要遵循受众国的文化习俗，又要在编写上做到准确、有趣，把中国故事讲好。

《风调雨顺：春夏秋冬》四册书法文化启蒙教材从酝酿到动笔撰写就花了近五年的时间，教材主要实验地在北美与南美部分学校，实验教材在使用过程中受到学生与教师的欢迎。该教材一方面介绍中国古代气象文化，以故事主人公中国妮妮给美国杰瑞讲故事的方式展开情节；另一方面，通过讲解汉字的构字特点来帮助不同文化背景的学生认知汉字里的文化，并采用二维码形式附上书法教学视频，方便实用，帮助学习者在书法、绘画、剪纸等艺术形式中加强对中国文化的整体理解。

感谢前联合国秘书长潘基文先生、上海交通大学张伟民教授、美国理海大学康妮教授、纽约大学唐力行教授、联合国国际学校孙青倩等老师在该教材编写过程中提出的中肯建议。感谢华东师范大学出版社王焰社长在教材出版过程中的大力支持。相信这四册“书法小联合国”汉字书法文化系列教材的顺利出版，会在中国书法文化国际教材开发中发挥积极的示范作用。

周斌于中国书法文化国际传播研究所

2017年10月28日

Postscript

Since the publication of *Let Me Write the Twelve Zodiac Signs* which belongs to the special course on calligraphy culture by United Association of Calligraphy in 2014, I have been receiving mails from parents and teachers from different schools all over the world. They asked me whether they could buy the video recordings of some demo lessons. And some of them encouraged me to keep writing more interesting calligraphy course books relevant to traditional Chinese culture.

It is not an easy task to compile a course book on calligraphy culture for overseas learners. Just as Rome was not built in a day, such a thin book of tens of pages also cannot be completed within a day. First of all, we need to find a suitable topic and its relevant materials. Then, we need to test the course book through continuous classroom instructions in various cultural contexts. After that we consult experts from all walks of life, and with feedback from classrooms, we finally make the decision to mass produce the course book. Our international course book series aim not only to suit the customs of the overseas learnes but also to tell the stories of Chinese culture with accuracy and amusement.

From the blueprint to the first draft of the four course books — *Spring/Summer/Fall/Winter: Season with Timely Breeze and Rain for Crop Raising* — for the enlightenment on Chinese calligraphy culture, it took us nearly five years to present them to the public. These course books were put on trial mainly in some schools in North and South America and got very positive feedback from both teachers and students. This course book series introduces Chinese people's understanding of the climate in ancient time through stories told by a Chinese character named Nini to an American character named Jerry. Furthermore, we have selected some ancient Chinese characters to help students from different cultural backgrounds get a better appreciation of the culture of Chinese characters. Moreover, we have attached a QR code in the part Practicing Calligraphy with Jerry. If you scan the QR code, you can watch videos teaching you how to write the characters. Learners' comprehensive understanding of Chinese culture will be improved by learning and practicing Chinese calligraphy.

Here I want to extend my sincere gratitude to the former UN Secretary-General, Mr Ban Ki-moon; Professor Zhang Weimin from Shanghai Jiao Tong University, Professor Connie from Lehigh University, and Professor Lixing Tang from New York University for their pertinent suggestions during the process of compiling these course books. I'm also grateful to president of East China Normal University Press, Mrs Yan Wang, for her substantial support during the publication process. I firmly believe that the publication of these four course books would play a very positive role in the development of international course books on Chinese calligraphy culture.

Zhou Bin

In Chinese Calligraphy Culture Education and Communication Center

28th October 2017

图书在版编目（CIP）数据

风调雨顺. 冬 / 周斌，周佳楠主编. —上海：华东师范大学出版社，2018
ISBN 978-7-5675-7959-0

Ⅰ. ①风… Ⅱ. ①周… ②周… Ⅲ. ①汉语－对外汉语教学－语言读物 Ⅳ. ① H195.5

中国版本图书馆 CIP 数据核字（2018）第 144091 号

风调雨顺 · 冬

主　　编　周　斌　周佳楠
策划编辑　王　焰
责任编辑　曹　琛
特约审读　曹一凡
责任校对　张多多
封面设计　刘怡霖

出版发行　华东师范大学出版社
社　　址　上海市中山北路 3663 号　邮编 200062
网　　址　www.ecnupress.com.cn
电　　话　021-60821666　行政传真　021-62572105
客服电话　021-62865537　门市（邮购）电话　021-62869887
地　　址　上海市中山北路 3663 号华东师范大学校内先锋路口
网　　店　http://hdsdcbs.tmall.com

印 刷 者　上海盛通时代印刷有限公司
开　　本　700×1000　12 开
印　　张　7
字　　数　49 千字
版　　次　2018 年 8 月第一版
印　　次　2018 年 8 月第一次
书　　号　ISBN 978-7-5675-7959-0/G · 11274
定　　价　48.00 元
出 版 人　王　焰

练习册使用说明

本书为《风调雨顺·冬》教材的配套练习册，希望通过二十四节气相关汉字的书法练习，使读者掌握书法学习的要领。本练习册通过对汉字字体笔顺和笔画的分析，为学习者掌握汉字的书写方法提供指导。同时，描红及空格练习也便于读者对照示范汉字进行反复书写。

This is the workbook for our course book *Winter: Season with Timely Breeze and Rain for Crop Raising*. We hope that readers will be able to master the principles of writing Chinese calligraphy after practicing the Chinese characters relevant to the Twenty-four Solar Terms. This workbook is going to give a detailed demonstration on strokes and the organization of these strokes in our sample characters, so as to provide a guidance of writing Chinese calligraphy for our learners. At the same time, the particular framework we offer in this workbook for learners to write in is very helpful because learners can practice repeatedly by imitating.

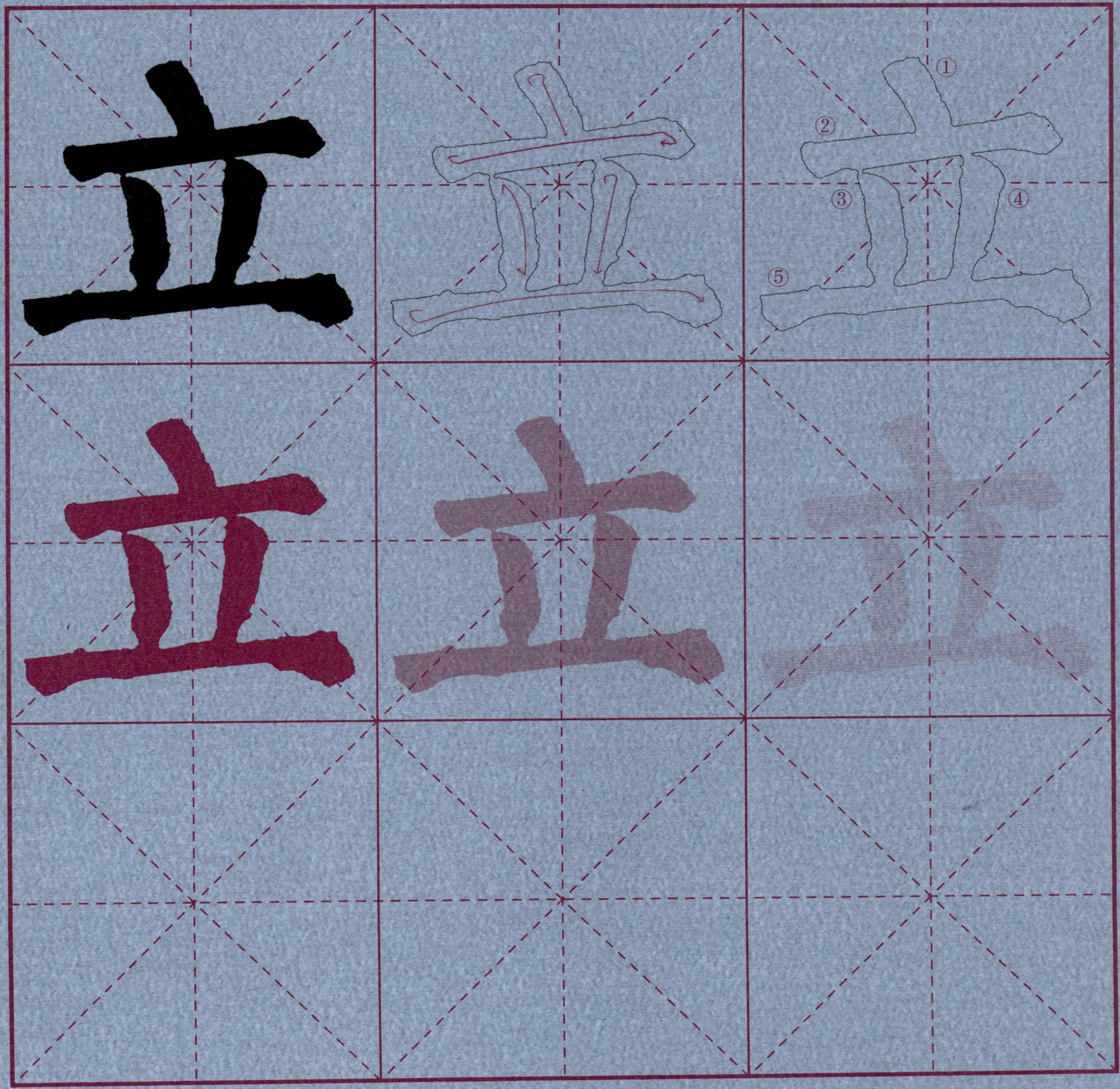
立
①
②
③
④
⑤

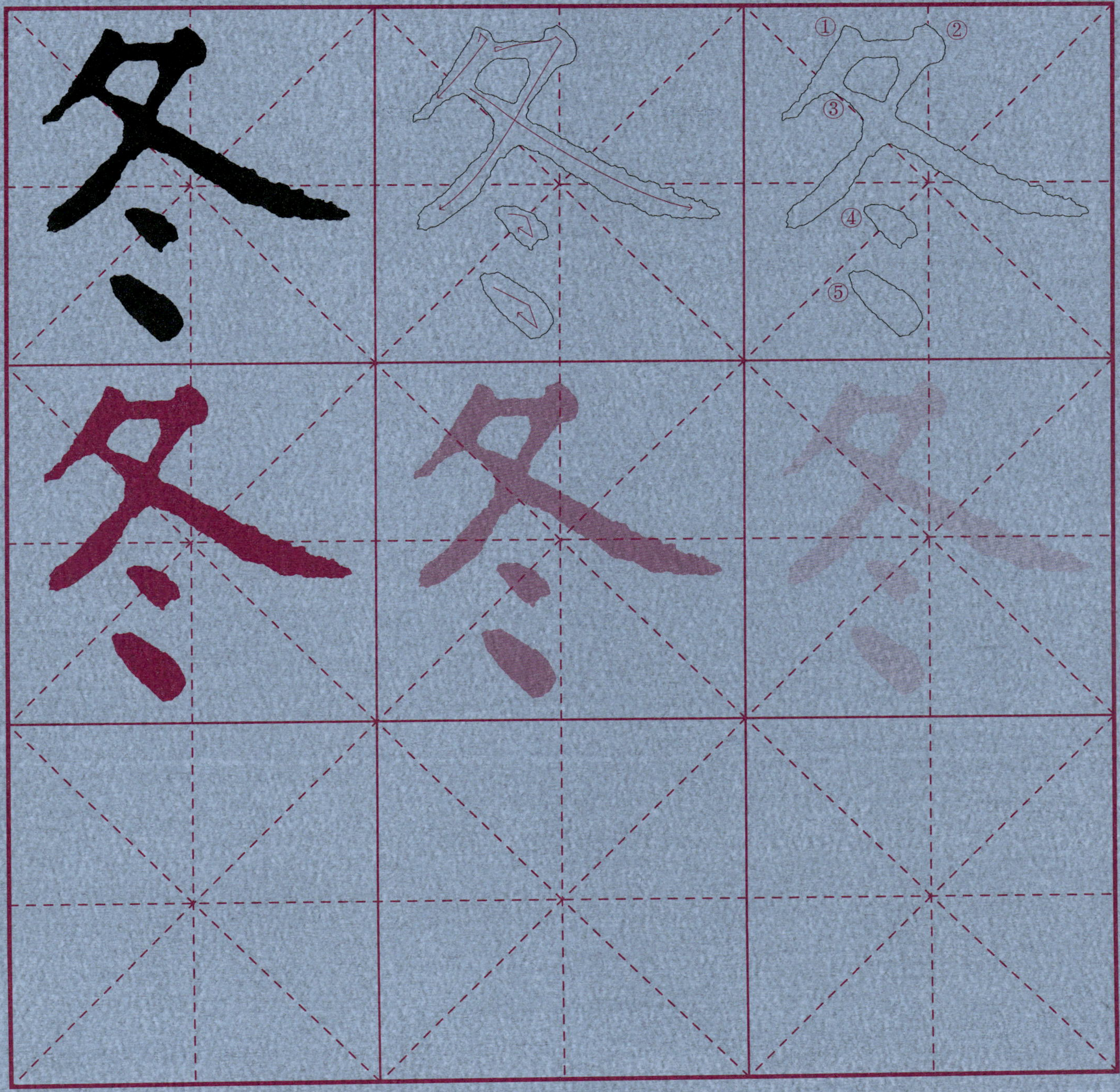
冬
①
②
③
④
⑤

小
①
②
③

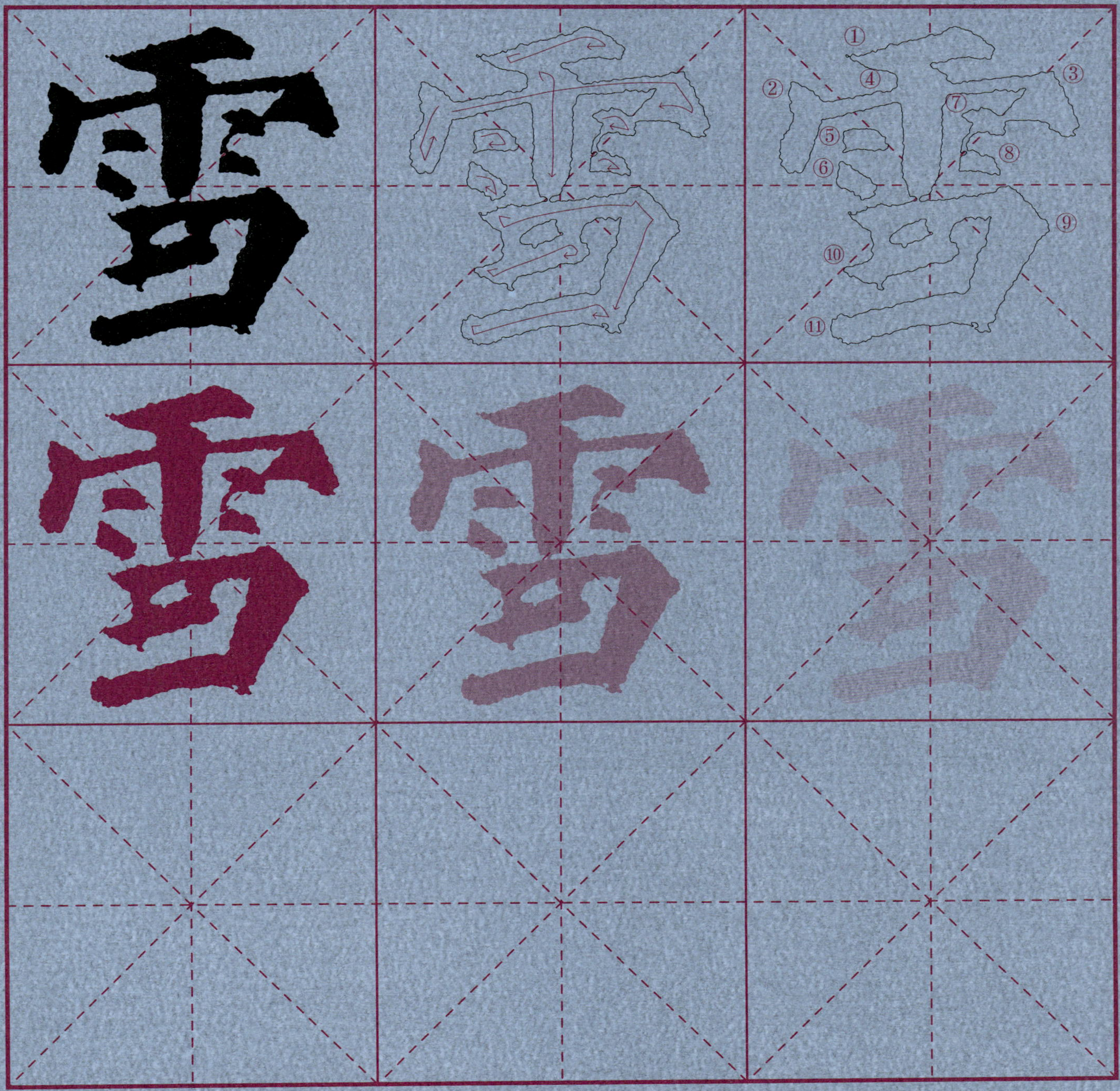
雪

大
②
①
③

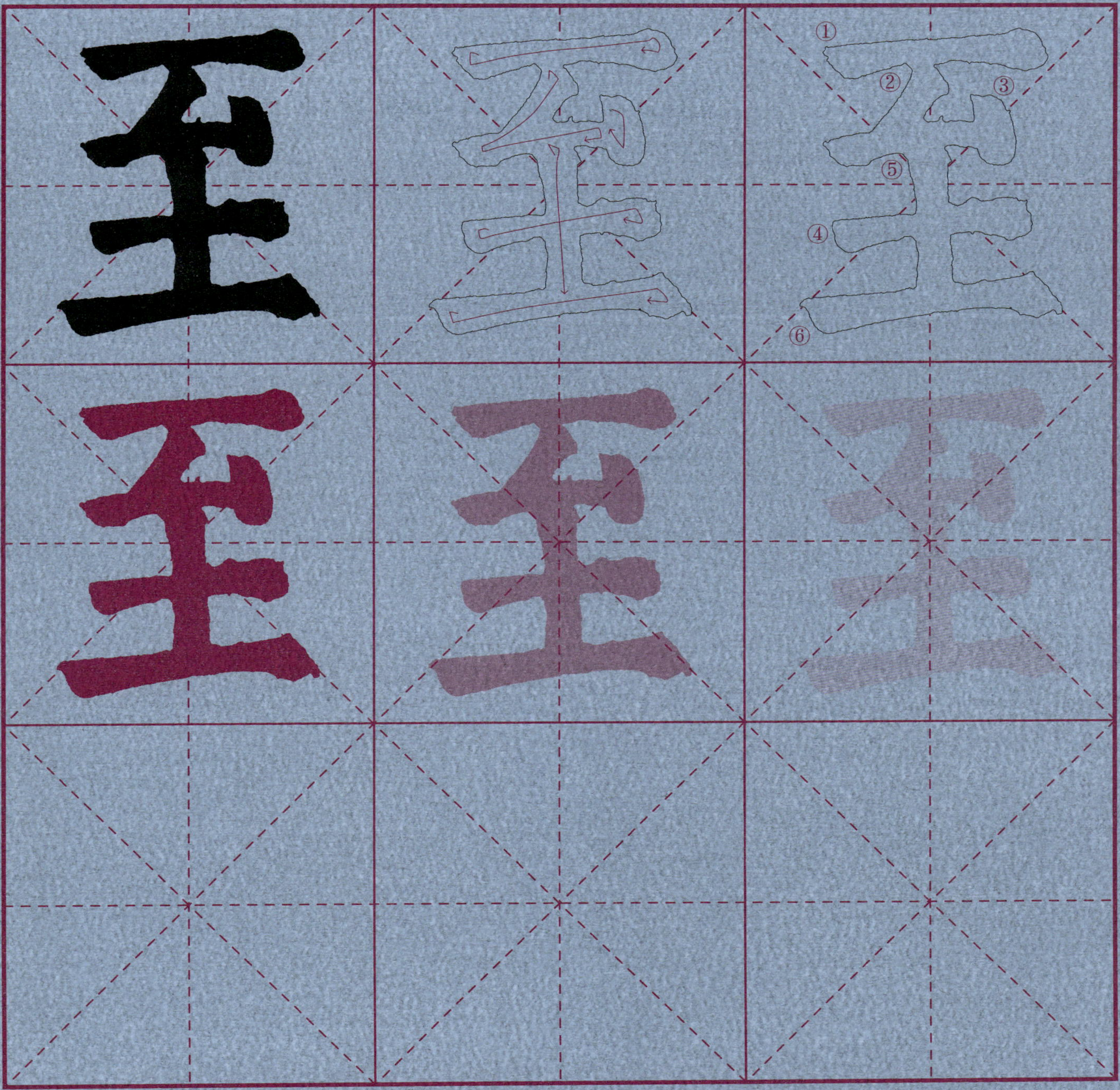
至

寒